"They're Gonna Settle Out of Court, Herman"

Other Herman Books

The 1st Treasury of Herman
The Second Herman Treasury
Herman, The Third Treasury
Herman: The Fourth Treasury
Herman Treasury 5
Herman, The Sixth Treasury
**"Herman, Dinner's Served ...
as Soon as the Smoke Clears!"**
**Herman, You Were a Much Stronger
Man on Our First Honeymoon**
The Latest Herman
**"Herman, You Can Get in
the Bathroom Now"**

"They're Gonna Settle Out of Court, Herman"

by Jim Unger

Andrews and McMeel
A Universal Press Syndicate Company
Kansas City • New York

ATTENTION: SCHOOLS AND BUSINESSES

"She makes all her own clothes."

"I thought you said you were in shipping."

5

"I'd like to return this mink. My husband
bought it for my birthday as a little joke."

"D'you wanna speak to the boss or to someone who knows what she's talking about?"

"His brother and his nephew Reggie are doing 12 years for armed robbery."

"Janice, I want a divorce."

7

"After you've finished the baby, I'd
like to change my name to 'Lance.'"

"How are you gonna defend me
if you can't stop laughing?"

"I'm sorry, sir, Dr. Rogers can
see you only by referral."

9

"It's an emergency. She's gotta be
at the hairdresser in three minutes."

"His dermatologist told him
to stay in the shade."

"Money or good looks attract me. I'd
say you'd need about $15 million."

"You won't find it under 'plumber.'
Look under 'drain surgeon.'"

11

"It's just as 'Goldie' left it
four years ago today."

"I'm gonna pay my electricity
bill while I'm here."

12

"He was born on the second
and third of December."

"I'm sorry, sir. You said you
wanted the cheapest room."

13

"These pills are a dollar each,
or you can take two for $1.50."

"Sure, you were good at it.
You were *there* for most of it."

14

"He's taking one of those correspondence courses to become a window dresser."

"She just had her physical. The doctor says she's as fit as a double bass."

"Our marriage was built on mutual
trust and a lot of acting ability."

"Sorry I left during your
sermon. I was sleepwalking."

16

"They're specially bred for long walks."

"It's so damp in our room, her wedding ring's turned green."

17

"If I pay this amount of taxes, I'll qualify for
tax exemption as a non-profit organization!"

"The honeymoon suite is booked
for another 20 minutes."

18

"I'll call you back in a couple of
days. I'm pretty busy right now."

"How much would it cost to send a 185-pound
wooden crate to Hawaii for two weeks?"

"Special delivery."

"Looks like 'zebra' finally made it onto the endangered list."

20

"That's my wife's lingerie."

"Well, now we know what they meant when they said, 'You can't take it with you.'"

"Can't you read?"

"We've genetically engineered a tuna exactly the same diameter as our cans."

"What am I . . . 48? That's the first time I
noticed my knees bend the other way!"

"I hope you're not one of those people
who has trouble swallowing pills."

"No, no, no. Point to Africa on the globe."

"Excuse me. May I go ahead of you? I'm in rather a hurry."

24

"My teacher assures me that even though I have your nose and eyes, genetics have absolutely nothing to do with the brain."

"Oh, that's nice. It says, 'Our company took every precaution to see that the pig didn't suffer.'"

"Have a cup of coffee
while I'm getting ready."

"When we get short of bed space,
we walk around the wards with it."

"This is the best I can do
for 'previous employment.'"

"Eighty years old and he doesn't
have a gray hair in his head."

"She coulda been Miss Universe
on any other planet."

"Did you have to buy him
such a big bucket?"

28

"Say, aren't you Harry Henderson
and Pete Watson?"

"I don't know what this is,
but you need a new one."

"Young man, has it occurred to you that you'll be boiling a young, innocent creature that would have had the potential for a full and productive life?"

"I gotta be straight with you, Andrea. I wear special shoes to make me look taller."

30

"I've done the best I can."

"Personally, I *prefer* a soft mattress."

"If you're bored, go home."

"Mom, is this my baby sitter?"

"I'b spled, I'b spill ab de benpisp."

"You should never stifle a sneeze!"

"I'm only really happy when I'm miserable."

"I need something with controls in the back seat."

"I can't wait to open your suitcase!"

"He didn't even notice my earrings!"

"He'd just spent $600
having his tooth capped."

"Sweetheart, don't forget
your school lunch."

"The fingerprint evidence is
pretty conclusive, your honor."

"Simpkins, how many times have I told you about using the office paper-shredder to make cole slaw?"

"I got them both during mating season."

"I had to give everyone their money back!"

"Someone stole his elevator shoes."

39

"Whaddyer mean, 'They don't look like you'? You *idiot.* They're *eggs!*"

"I need a pair of dancing shoes with steel-toe caps."

"If you touch that nerve again, I'm gonna teach you a new meaning for the word *pain*."

"You know what they say, 'Two can starve as cheaply as one.'"

41

"You promised me you'd get a haircut."

"We've just walked two miles ... that's 14 for him."

42

"For the last *&*% time . . . over
the wire fence is *not* a home run."

"Whadda you think of gun control?"

43

"He loves people. But mostly
he gets canned dog food."

"My birthday surprise was walking into the
kitchen and finding the toaster on fire."

44

"You'll have to return to your seat, sir
...we can't keep circling the airport."

"He gets those sudden migraines."

"Take that out of your mouth and tell the nice man why you'd like a job here."

"I always sit behind her on the bus in case there's a head-on collision."

"It keeps the bag-snatchers away."

"No wonder you're having difficulty walking. You've got an armchair back here!"

"You told me to hang your mother's picture in the hallway."

"I thought you said they'd fixed this thing!"

"This is the 11th time I've sent you to prison. You haven't learned much in 30 years, have you?"

"I didn't say 'undress.' I said 'address.'"

"Can I eat half of all I can eat for $3.50?"

"Since she got her new teeth,
she's put on 60 pounds."

"I taught him everything
I know and he's still stupid."

"What's it like for cornering?"

"Would you say you're 'dogmatic'?"

"Is that all you have to say in your defense?"

"How often do you find a basement apartment with a balcony?"

"I'm taking you off the vitamins for a while."

"I wanted to get you a gift you deserved,
but they didn't have anything cheaper!"

"Get me to the airport in 10 minutes
and I *may* overlook this filthy cab."

"I don't think Mom makes
spaghetti on toast like that."

"I don't want to rush things.
Let's exchange photographs first."

"It happened during one of those used-car dealer commercials."

"Which hospital did you stay at on your honeymoon?"

"Got the waterproof matches?"

CUSTOMER SERVICE

"The guarantee ran out while you were on the phone."

58

"Here's your supper. I've waxed the floor."

"My doctor told me to take a cruise and relax."

59

"They're all the same. . . . As soon
as I laid the egg, he was off."

"Send the speeding ticket to the
car lot. I'm not buying it."

"Come back and see me in two
weeks, and don't wear that tie."

"Quit fooling around!"

"OK, a cheeseburger for you. What about the Statue of Liberty over here?"

"So this is your private box at the theater!"

62

"Whaddyer mean, 'Don't get mad at him'? He bought a diamond necklace for his girlfriend with *my* credit card!"

"Rapid pulse, sweating, shallow breathing. . . . According to the computer, you've got gallstones."

"I'd like to bury your daughter."

"I wouldn't pay all that for a dress while you're still growing."

"It serves him right. He's bitten the valve off my tire!"

"You're *supposed* to be holding it *straight!*"

"Your cousin Ernie failed
his skydiving course."

"We'll get you down to
X-ray in a few minutes."

67

"If I can't spell it, how can I
look it up in the dictionary?"

"I'm just going over to the
bowling alley to get a candy bar."

"I lost 10 pounds once. To be honest,
I didn't notice any difference."

"You're OK. How am I?"

"Go and open the front door while your mother's cooking. I don't want the fire department breaking it down with an ax."

"It's nothing to worry about, but I want you to wear this Medic-Alert helmet."

70

"Most of them are for ballroom dancing."

"My school report card is not going to help your ulcer."

"She's the only one who can
eat her own cooking."

"I wish you hadn't told the
waiter he didn't look his age."

"I bought her a cookbook the day we got married. . . . It's still in the wrapper."

"Wouldn't I get faster service if I slept in your room?"

73

"You'd look a lot better if you didn't wear a striped shirt."

"You never seen a ham operator before?"

"She went to see a hypnotist to lose weight and he put on 40 pounds."

"A lot of men would *love* to be 7 feet tall."

"See what happens when you can't
make up your mind?I . . . 'Illegal U-Turn.'"

"How many times have I told you
about running in the corridors?"

"There's a bottle of wine on here that's more than our mortgage payment!"

"One size fits all."

"We've been married for 27 years. How about time off for good behavior?"

"Stand back, everybody. He thinks he's a frog."

"He says he's invented a saltshaker
that will never clog."

"I wanna say, 'take your job
and shove it' in poinsettias."

"His doctor told him to stay
away from anything fatty."

"I guess you could say I'm a self-made man."

"We just don't see eye to eye anymore."

"My ex-husband was up all
night buying everybody drinks."

"This will all be yours one day, Darryl."

"Needless to say, we don't buy
the extra-large eggs anymore."

"We've been married more than
seven months now, Beryl. Shouldn't
you be ironing or something?"

"She gave me aftershave for Christmas,
so I gave her beauty soap."

"It's not as bad as it looks."

"You can call me apathetic if you like. See how much I care!"

"He's looking for something for the woman who has nothing."

"This reading lamp hasn't uttered a word since I bought it!"

"Stay away from that cake in the fridge."

"I wonder if they spray chemicals on macaroni."

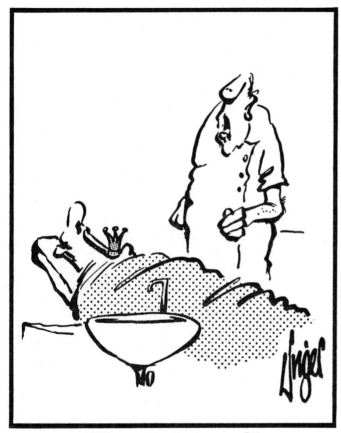

"Who put in that crown?"

" 'Catch of the Day' is fish fingers."

"It's for my mother-in-law.
Got anything rabid?"

"Yes, yes, I know you were excited.
But read it yourself. It says, 'Head
man wanted for branch office.'"

"Your honor, if my client is found not guilty, he could lose more than $2 million in book royalties alone."

"I brought your slippers."

"I'm only helping with the dishes
'til you get your pacemaker."

"Take me to the best restaurant in
town and leave the engine running."

"Harold, the doctor made you quit the insurance office because you kept bringing your work home."

"She wants to know what the pot roast was like."

91

"I can't remember which one of these is fish
and chips and which one is liver and onions."

"What's the get-well card for?"

"I warned you about pulling out gray hairs."

"It'll speed things up if
you order the meatloaf."

"You get a company car after two years."

"What is it this time?"

"Sure I'll take you out to dinner!
Which two restaurants?"

"Whaddyer mean, 'I burnt the
oatmeal'? . . . that's coffee!"

95

"I'm studying astrophysics and you're reading me *Goldilocks and the Three Bears*!"

"I just want to tell everyone that up until this moment, I've really enjoyed working here."

"Mother asked me to get you to open this jar of pickles for her."

"He's been driving 16 hours non-stop."

"Personally, I think it helps the divorce
if we leave *both* of them in there."

"Listen, friend, if you wanna
date my daughter, you'd better
start letting your hair grow."

"I heard you played by ear."

"Pepper?"

"I missed the gas pedal."

"We haven't had a contract since 1742!"

"The dog ate a whole bag of chili powder."

"Have you got that book, *How to Be Six Feet Tall Under Hypnosis?*"

"No, thanks. I couldn't take your last nickel."

"Are you steering?"

"Grandma, can you lend me $11 to get a set of false fingernails?"

"Remember the good old days when the railway porter used to put down a little wooden step to help you get off the train?"

"You should be careful with blisters. You'd better let the doctor take a look at it."